Additional Praise for *Hunger*

"Alice Derry's poetry is nourished not only by the
celebrations and joys of life—travel to Greece, a deep
and abiding knowledge of world literature, a poignant
relationship with the natural world—but by the
complexities of living within these very relationships.
The continual presence of loss, suffering, injustice—that
we, as humans, must face—carry these poems into their
fullest realization. The 'unravel[ling]' of expectation—
and of longing—as a kind of 'freedom' is the heart of
Hunger and its continual fulfillment. This is the freedom
to be nourished, sustained by our living itself."
—Kate Reavey, author of *Too Small to Hold You*

D1736522

HUNGER

HUNGER

poems by
Alice Derry

MoonPathPress

Poetry

ISBN 978-1-936657-29-2

Cover art painting, *The White of Air*, is by Josie Gray, gouache on paper.

Author photo by Lisel and Ron Murdock-Perriera.

Design by Tonya Namura using Baskerville.

MoonPath Press is dedicated to publishing the finest poets of the U.S. Pacific Northwest.

MoonPath Press

PO Box 445

Tillamook, OR 97141

MoonPathPress@gmail.com

http://MoonPathPress.com

Also by Alice Derry

Tremolo
Rainer Rilke: Selected New Poems (translations)
Strangers to their Courage
Clearwater
Not as You Once Imagined
Getting Used to the Body
Stages of Twilight

Acknowledgments

Many thanks to the periodicals and anthologies in which some of these poems originally appeared, some in earlier forms:

Hunger: *Catamaran*

Closing In: *Crab Creek Review*

Doors: *Coal Hill Review*

Trio Petra: traveling *Crosscurrents* exhibit (Washington Community College Humanities Association): appeared in the galleries of Washington Community Colleges

Autumn: Second Flowering: *Crosscurrents* of WCCHA

Black Hawk: *Flint Hill Review*

Along the Columbia River Highway: *Floating Bridge Review*

Giving my Daughter *The Scarlet Letter*: *Floating Bridge Review*

Jury Duty: *Floating Bridge Review*

Trumpeter: *Floating Bridge Review*

Shelter: *Great River Review*

White: *Great River Review*

Heartsick: *Hubbub*

Nolde: *Hubbub*

Horse Fantasies: *Ploughshares*

Dieskau: *Poets Unite! The Lit Fuse @10 Anthology*

Listening to Stone: *Plume*

A Hawk: *Poetry East*

Camouflage: *Poetry East*

The Extravagance of Our Longing: *Poetry East*
Big Hole: *Windfall*
Lower Lights: *Windfall*
Wind Turbines: *Windfall*

As a chapbook, *The Extravagance of Our Longing* was a runner-up in the Coal Hill Review Chapbook contest.

My deepest gratitude to Charlotte Warren, who guided these poems to completion over many years of rich discussion. My great thanks to Joseph Powell, who worked on the manuscript more than once. Thanks also to Kate Reavey for her feedback on the poems. I am indebted to Tess Gallagher for her insightful comments toward final revision and continuing nourishment of my writing life. I thank Lisel Mueller for support of my work over long years. Many thanks to Kevin Miller, whose letters helped me in a hard time, and to friends and colleagues who have sustained me. Thanks to Jane Mead and Molly Gloss for their support of the poems. Thanks to Josie Gray, my cover artist and friend. And thank you, Lana, for keeping poetry in the public eye and believing in these poems.

always the ones, Bruce and Lisel

and for Ron, for Ronan

I have a want on me.

—Josie Gray

What if God created hunger in God's image?
What if God is hunger? Tell me, how do you
pray to hunger? How do you ask for hunger's
blessing? How will hunger teach you to forgive?
How will hunger teach you how to love?

—Sherman Alexie

Table of Contents

HUNGER

I

This Far Along

Does hunger provide a kind of infinity?

—Mark Irwin on Kafka
(*American Poetry Review*)

Heartsick

at twelve. *This close to dying,*
our doctor said. I couldn't feel death,
except I lay in a hospital room

without my mother,
the nurses of the fifties treating
rheumatic fever as a venial sin.

Half a century later, a dozen or more ravens
tuck under this ridge, disappear.
Quorks and grunts thicken the air.

They've left me in a field of huckleberries—
scarlet leaves, threaded
with frost. Once I've climbed the first hill,

their black arrow divides the October sky
in total silence. If I weren't looking,
I wouldn't know to look.

On this trail I have by heart
each turn reveals the next thing
I can't explain.

We think we command the body
but Prince Andrei, dying of his war wounds
in *War and Peace*, turned his eyes

away from the woman he loved, the one
he'd fastened them on for weeks,
desire no longer tonic.

Silence. Call. Call and echo.
Heart's work—respond.
The ravens scream down the valley below me.

Recovery didn't mean I got my mother back.
The heart, well, couldn't do more
than urge, *Keep going.*

And soon I'm over the ridge, remembering
the hand- and foot-holds, clambering
across the broken shale to the edge.

Whatever weather arrives by afternoon
will stay, wind from the west hurrying clouds
as they roll over Mt. Olympus.

My mother turned from me long before
I was twelve. After the prince died,
I had pages and pages to read without him.

Absence rises like lines from a poem
we half remember. Words leave their source,
and in their new landscape, speak differently.

One footfall of my boots after another
beats hollow on the hard dirt of this trail.
Passage, bountiful and severe.

Nolde

After many of his works were seized by the Nazis,
in 1941 Emil Nolde was forbidden to paint.

1

Begging them to let him continue,
he made mistakes. The worst perhaps
his groveling, *really, he'd always been*
their supporter. That letter can't be erased.

We don't fault him that his *colors*
are extreme, like the one scarlet
dahlia opening in my ruined garden
this frosted morning—

My eye pinioned by red
except when it's pulled
to the thistle's Prussian blue.

One woman's cheeks and forehead seared
flame yellow, another's throat
patched crimson—the Nazis
could see too well these faces
argued a scalding geography.

2

Anchored by green-black foreboding
he brushes into a slumping barn,
color leaps to violet and orange.
They masquerade as sky.

His lightest green stops me,
tips of waves right before they go too far,
black undersides of breakers like fear.

We blame him that when forced
to words, he could only describe
how he loved his country.

3
Inside these watercolors, I could know him.
Each day, forbidden, cutting
precious paper smuggled in by friends,
cutting it small, cutting up the old paintings too
for their reverse sides,

and there, deep in the house he could
never believe silent, the colors' fluency
loud as betrayal, he laid down first one,
then the next, as he always had,

until their layers and mixings sprang up
as light, or deadened. The failed ones
were still. The others he hushed, turning them
to the wall. *Not now*, he'd say. *Not yet.*

This Far Along

nothing but wind.
It shifts the thick sheets of overcast back and forth,
wrapping them more firmly around us, as we
crunch through sand and shingles,
foam breaking from a china blue
rare once the sky's lost its bright offer.
Upland, rain has tarnished the ripened beach grass.
We walk arm in arm, mother and daughter,
not clinging, but a metaphor for clinging,
light touch of catch and release
standing in for all the years we mirrored each other.
Now we live in the resemblance
of that life, a few shared experiences
at intervals and the past remembered
so differently, my own childhood the smoldering coals
I can touch to flame
while yours, the one we lived together, recedes,
and you tell it to me with the same
ferocious sharpness of fiction.
What I've asked for has happened,
your mind quickened far beyond me
as one day you moved in my body
already swollen and dulled by hormones
which said *stay* and *accumulate,*
and that was the beginning of separation.
Your arms encircle me, benign
protection I've begun to count on.
After our beach day, winter dusk gives the old permission
to settle against me on the couch,
as you once did. Or the vivid landscapes
of your bad dreams bring you to my bed.
We curl together, still each other.

Trumpeter

for Sara

The class practices on cadaver birds.
Moving among the tables, helping,
the biologist tells how she once
found a trumpeter swan
trapped in a barbed wire fence.
She cut it free, took it home. Sinking her hands
into the feathered layers and finding the shoulder
only badly sprained, instinctively

she massaged, the giant bird relaxing
into her arms. It snaked its long neck over her shoulder
and down her back like the heavy comfort
of her childhood braid, until, bill resting
on her waist, it fell asleep, gently snoring.

Two days she fed the swan in her bathtub,
returning it to the fence where its mate
unbelievably waited. She couldn't help
watching as the pair lingered for days
until the shoulder opened wings to flight—
reading the invisible, secret landings,
re-entry—a mysterious map the biologist

hopes to glimpse. When she raises her eyes,
she finds her listeners have lured her story on,
even as she's instructed their hands
to intubate the cadavers, band their legs,
register and photograph them.

We've got to have this information first,
she remembers, *for the lawsuit.*

I listen as Sara tells me each detail,
thinking, yes, that's how it happens in rape cases,
first the doctor's probing,
so charges can be brought.

The biologist's tone
makes a bird saved less important
than the news each evening this spring,
delivering a pelican pulling its great blackened wings
like a crucifixion through the BP oil.

Past cadavers now, the class works
on practice ducks. The biologist assists.
But her story is the only reason they're here.

Just as a mother closes her arms around
her daughter, released from the exam at last,
in an emergency,

these class members will cradle oiled birds,
self to self,
soap their blackened feathers, letting heated air
stream to the cleaned inner down, while the birds,
half-asleep, waken and begin to preen.

Even in the shock of ordeal, some can summon
their body's waterproofing, wings braced
for the long swoop and fall of evening
across the roughened Pacific.

Wind Turbines

No one knew the color of the sky.
Stephen Crane

Joe, we didn't lie down on this ground to save it.
When bulldozers churned these flats above Ellensburg,
concrete pads sprouting towers to blot the sky,
I didn't drive over the pass in solidarity. The turbine blades
hum so tenderly, rising high as coastal firs above us,
their blades rhythmic machetes against the air, I'm lulled,

unafraid. Bent to the ground, how easily I erase
what I don't want to be there. We're combing the dozers'
unearthed bounty, agates pocketed in cooling lava
from an earlier age. You've hunted stones
for thirty years. I stare at the uniform clay
while you press fragment after fragment into my hand.

In all this wind and humming, I've lost my husband
and daughter. We went out together, but people
get stubborn, each wanting their own search. I trot
to keep up with you. *The citizen meetings took
months*, you say. *We agreed on other land for the turbines,
but the governor overrode us—someone had her ear.*

I look up to meet your scorn. The hills interrupt me,
still there, golden with cheat grass, gradually
muted in sagebrush's gray. Higher, islands of pine
paint the dark contrast. Huge sky—thunderheads
rear, then stretch thin, like the flared tails of plunging
horses. A few drops sizzle but mostly wind

flattening grass to the scalp of the rise. It smothers our talk.
Like the girl I once was in Montana, I let it heave
against me, stream past, so I can find my people.
Wind pulls the tears from me. *Sure,* I say, but I'm almost
yelling. *Someone looked out here and said,*
There's nothing. Great place for turbines!

Jury Duty

This accused in his crisp blue shirt,
slighter than I am,
continually running his hand

through his dark, cropped hair,
would be crushed in prison.
I know from my students—

freely admitting their guilt,
they've written of the violence
used against them.

He stares into space
beside his defense attorney,
whose suit is too tight, shoes scuffed.

The prosecutor's on her feet,
apologizing for taking
our last day of summer,

grilling us, nineteen prospective jurors,
about our experiences
with drinking and driving.

One woman raises her hand,
a felony assault.
The next explains, *my alcoholic husband*

tried to run me off the road,
but he mistook a different car for mine.
It was another woman he left to die.

A third's nephew
has been *rendered quadriplegic.*
I turn from the defendant

to their stories, willing to carry them
as I'm seated in the box.
But the prosecutor strikes me

from duty, along with my fellow juror,
pushing from behind
as we leave, breathing,

Whew, we got out of that one.
Who'd work hard for a guy
who refused a breathalyzer test?

I drive into my free afternoon.
When the prosecutor had asked
what could make a person refuse the test,

I speculated, *Maybe the policeman*
didn't treat him well—
just rounding up ideas, keeping

Rodney King in mind, or more recently,
Henry Louis Gates, Junior—all of us,
of course, white in this small town

courtroom on our country's western edge—
Why didn't I leap to the answer
everyone in the room except me

seemed to know, so that needing
no voice, it rose out of the combined air
and fell like a scolding—

Only the guilty, those in the fog of drink,
would refuse. That I shouldn't be
standing on the slippery ground

at the crime scene, a night thick
with rain, or even spangled in stars,
forming their sure alliances,

while I listened to the talk
of two frightened men,
one wearing the badge we'd given him.

Hunger

beginning with words from Wallace Stevens

Sunday mornings in childhood, rising early
for scant toast and chocolate, she was handed
words—two services and an hour of Bible study—
to blunt the sharp rise of her hunger
until it dulled to a steady hum of want.
Her mother, sustained all day, giddy really,
on faith, returned to the small pot roast
reluctantly, hours later doling it out to eight.

Once the girl had left home, Sunday mornings,
completely hers, became the late sleep
on a weekend's second day—ample breakfasts
cooked in the mind of angled light
soaking the kitchen, iris and rose of her garden
where she idled, setting the beds straight.
Rain days too, gazing into the steep canyon,
green and light-green, colors' dependency.

Why would the call of color be so great
if she had nothing of the dance in her?
How contrast lifts an image from two dimensions
and sets it whirling across a room!
She allowed herself expensive colored pencils,
boxes of watercolor—or bought
them for her own daughter, who sighted
along a still life and made it live on paper.

Rain now, in fact, in the misty stands
of ocean spray, hazelnut, and huckleberry,
damping the violet slash of swallows.
Seeing and light. But not the hand
which translates scene to paint. Along the path,
she fingers the sawed edge of a rose leaf,
its blood-red unfolding gradually into green.
Dusk returns her to the house.

Listening to rain under lamplight
brings words as themselves, rising
with their Biblical rhythms past the burden
of evangelical warning, to sound onto her page,
highlighting a person's features, shading
an early summer landscape. One hunger,
another. She can start soup, make bread.
Eat enough. She doesn't have to wait.

In Brooklyn

a reading of James Wright's "A Blessing"

for Max and for his teacher

1

First time, bicycling Cobble Hill:
I steer the thin gauntlet between traffic and parked cars,
afraid the door of one of these stilled vehicles
will push open. My legs, obedient
to keeping balance, press the bike forward—
how our friend once lay broken on the street.

Veering instead from a dead rat, sun-glistening,
fine-haired coat. I surge past—*don't let me
fall here*—eyes not allowed to flinch—
its insides, pressed out whole,
cherries ripe on black pavement.

2

In the 4th grade classroom, Max wants to—read
your poem out loud, James Wright. He can't even
say all the words, the brain he's been given ebullient
with what's possible, but no match
for the slick roadway rushing onward
where print meets sound.

Even in front of the fluent reader next to him,
obsessed with perfection—*he missed "the"*—
in front of me, the visiting poet,
Max wants to read "A Blessing."

With her softly-spoken helps, his teacher
keeps him upright as he pedals, each word
nuzzling our outstretched hands
to *ripple* in darkness,

how your poem's passage through struggle
has lightened it,

you'd be astonished, James Wright.
The children hold five fingers
tight as buds
until the teacher repeats *blossom*,
and the petals push open.

3
I want to stay steady, reach the East River,
see it fill with flood-tide *face to face*—
as Whitman predicted our crossings, I stand
on Brooklyn's shore, use his words to answer—
Where I stop, your ferry crossed.

Under red-gold October of Brooklyn, a rat's shattering.
Everything has to be in view to keep from crashing,
all the *beautiful ministers* which *furnish* their part.
We fathom you not, Whitman writes, fearless
with overstatement. *We plant you permanently
within us.*

Print to sound—as much like a plant's
blind reach for bloom and seed as anything—
Max felt his way and let us see his feeling.

II

Stealing from Young Women

700,000 women and children are trafficked worldwide each year

When I first met him [my pimp], I desperately needed attention. He showed me attention. I loved it [. . . .] I had to meet with clients always, even if I was sick or the weather was terrible. I couldn't get off the street until I brought home $1000 [. . . .] I was locked in a room and whipped with an electrical cord because I didn't bring in enough money. Because I resisted his beatings and that scared him, I was beaten so thoroughly, I was hospitalized. My mother called the police. They made the situation worse, demanded what I couldn't give [. . . .] I ran for eleven months. I was in jail for nine months. I lost my son at six and a-half months [. . . .] Look for girls who have no stability or anyone to hold their hands through school; look for girls moving past their parents.

—notes from a lecture given
by a Seattle-area woman
forced into prostitution.

Stealing from Young Women

lessons and carols at Advent

1

In a country not far
from the original Eden, a husband
has held his own wife down,
had her nose and ears cut off.

We've brought her here.
Over months, doctors re-fashion
her features, opening her memory
with each stroke of their knives.

Healing, says the radio,
like the Baptist of our times,
a bodiless voice *crying in the wilderness.*

Then I leave my car
to sit with my youngest brother
in the pews, as we used to,
Sunday after Sunday.

His teenager sings the deepest bass
in this boy choir, harmonizing
familiar carols. In between,
we hear the season's lessons:
Yes, Eve says simply, *I ate*,
hiding behind no one
when her husband blames her.

Trying to take charge of her life.

Within hours after the twelve-year old
runaway turned to a gang member

for help, she was his, servicing
ten to fifteen customers a day,
the money less risky than drug trafficking.

She's safe now, the radio reporter added.
From what?

2
The next young man reads Luke:
Troubled when the angel visits, Mary
cast in her mind what manner of salutation
this should be.

No different from Zeus
in his waddling disguise as swan.

The writer of Genesis imagined
the garden as lushness
in a confluence of two rivers.
And I think of the good sex
I've had with my husband.
Bodies for a moment stilled,
but slippery enough, we fit
into the hollows of shoulders
and thighs, one self, making
the sleepy talk of comfort.
That straightforward.

3
After my clear child soprano lowered
to alto, I couldn't hear the harmony.
Wanting to sing in the church choir herself,
Mother let me slip into the pews.
Onto my lap and to my sides,

she placed my three small brothers,
carols our thin blanket.

Years of being a mother
when I wasn't one. The December
this brother lay in the Christmas manger,
they dressed me as the virgin.

Behold, Mary finally concedes
to the persistent angel, his hand
over the mouth of all her questions,
Behold the handmaid of the lord.

Stealing from young women.

I still have to remind myself,
I have a right to my life.

4
Today I'm just *passing* in this church,
as light-skinned Blacks speak of passing.

Behind what I mouth, mild December
dusk, sun careening barely
above the mountains, garden
without metaphor, buds ready
for late spring sun in the copses, sap.

I don't know—the world may hold
something more than we perceive.
What stands in plain view:
it took my friend twenty years
to leave the husband who beat her
mercilessly, four children watching
while she went back again and again.

Giving My Daughter *The Scarlet Letter*
thinking of Lisel Mueller's poem

Five years older than
you are now—that's when I
first read it—

and since have taught it many times—
clearly, without hesitation,
presenting Dimmesdale
as Hawthorne's example
of moral weakness—

Since you were born—and after all, Dimmesdale
had a daughter too—
he's the type I can hardly stand,
leaving a woman to bear alone
what they've made together—
we know how common it is.

(Shame, of course—I'm not making light
of what single mothers still bear,
but Hester had her Pearl, just as I have you,
out of her love, a person she'd
get to spend years with.)

I'm losing my point,
something you often accuse me of.
When I first read *The Scarlet Letter*,
I'm saying, I tried to defend Dimmesdale.

I wanted to preserve him for Hester.
Play over the last forest scene
where they pledge themselves to each other
again. They could work things out.

My professor, usually so indulgent,
simply said, "No. That's not there,
not in the text at all." I withdrew,
but kept my idea, secretly.

Now, offering the book to you,
those days flood back.
I was just learning love myself,
to love the man we never speak of,

my first husband. He drew me in,
as Hester was drawn, so willingly,
a thirst which could never
be slaked, my whole gift of passion.
And then said *no*.

Like Dimmesdale, he hid.
From his father, who tried to beat it
out of him. From his mother,
from me, the person he was hiding behind.
While he worked late and found ways
to meet his men.

In the end, as I've told you,
sin having reached such high regard
in our country, dispersed from Hester's narrow town—
I could leave a marriage for my own good.
That much of the story is clear to you.

Just that people haven't let go of the shame.
A scared man wrecks a life,
trying to save his own.

Making love, drowsing together
in a hotel in Italy, maybe the last night
I could trust myself to drift
in someone's warmth,
suddenly he was shaking me.
I need a divorce.

Not that long, you understand,
after I had tried to make *The Scarlet Letter*
predict our future—every emotion
understated to searing heat.

That her great ardor had fallen
on a disguised life.

White

This far toward summer,
grown girls shiver into their frosty gowns,
gauze and veil, braving dangerous lives.

Hidden in the lavish outpour of June,
winter's word feels safe,
borne against a bride's exposed skin.

Starched dogwood, giant parsnip,
thimbleberry's well-worn muslin
dazzle the roadside tangles, blinding,

as a girl presses through the thick snow
of this field's wild daisies.
Sun-deep in them, how could she go under?

Black Hawk

living our lives through the radio

1.

At his base, through an interpreter,
he learns that these children he's rescued
watched their parents being shot—
a girl, seven, boy, six, shrapnel in their bodies.

He strokes her face, her hair. Like any dad.
All night she calls for her mother.
When he gives her pain medication,
her eyes insist: *I need my mother.*

In the morning his Black Hawk team
readies for its next medical mission.
The children will go to a Baghdad hospital.
She clings to him. He holds her.
I kissed her on the cheek. I let her go.

2.

South of Europe, a woman
is tricked into crossing a border.
Sold. Fifteen men a day

forced onto her. The radio
narrates a story possible
only because her husband

refused to be caught
in the web of payoffs
and police cover-ups.

He rescued her. *Rescue*
from French and Latin,
to shake off again. And again.

This woman and I both wake
to a morning washed in new light.
She struggles from the sheets,

stands in her pristine gown,
spoiled by sweat.
Only her days are free.

Last night I was suddenly staring
into what could only be
innocent dark.

Just a dream, I comforted
myself. Through a window,
men discover me.

They are closing in.
I try to call for my husband.
I try to get out of bed and run.

To shake violently, that's what
jerks me awake—
from the same Latin as *rescue.*

3.

Myriam Merlet: her voice
buried in the earthquake's rubble.

She chastised her own people—
rape can't be a political weapon,
or *business as usual.*

Nights among the wounded,
what speaks is the silence of children,
already aware that crying is futile.

In a compound, mothers
circle their girls. Freed
by earthquake, rape stalks
any female crossing to the latrine.

As I drive my country roads, the car
heater reaching its warmth, a man's voice
cries, *I have lost my children, lost them.*

In the nameless way of mass graves.
Not a word remains.

From the women, singing, inchoate,
gains strength, rising as it must have
two centuries ago around campfires
when slaves began to murmur and plan—
Haitians would free *themselves.*

Inchoate, Latin, *to hitch up.*

The women sing to get started,
their complex harmony brought to bear
against humans hitched to plows,
humans plowed like fields.

Tender

When the men drift away, the women begin
to speak their pain. How it keeps them awake nights,
that their doctors have prescribed this and that.
They don't complain—as if suffering rose
without cause and infused them,
sun soaking this pasture after rain,
releasing scent. Around these words,

we hover near Sara's tailgate set with snacks,
hands warming on tea cups. A pair of ravens tramps
through air like solid ground.
Eagles building a nest this spring
pushed them farther along the hogback.
They're still objecting.

Volunteers, we've only known each other
these summer weeks, but as we amble back to weed,
daylighting the newly-planted oak trees,
the women's talk, like allowance,
frees your story, Rachel—

losing your brother when he was eight,
losing your mother's listening then too.
Put my ashes there—she told you on your last visit,
pointing to the big cedar at the field's edge—
where his play was happiest—
although you steadied her across the field.

No matter how high you hold it,
the black salamander you've found,
green stripe down its two-inch back,
tries to jump from your hand
to its grasses and seeps, its familiar.

Something allows the hidden
to surface in us, a strike of light or the distraction
of small animals. Nothing contiguous, except
that we guard these moments against indifference,
waiting for a listener.

No child of the six in my family died,
but our mother left us as surely as yours,
her attention fixed elsewhere.

What a close family we have, our parents said,
annulling any words for absence.
The salamander tips from your hand into the grass.

I don't tell you that story when you turn for my answer
because all morning a woman's hand has been
in front of me—from last night's TV.
I tell you that a person can refuse to pass on depravity,
that tenderness, like the assertion
of sun into a field, takes up substance
at that very moment—

tender, I say—how, her body immobile from injury,
the woman still reaches her hand
to cup the curled head of her toddler
who clutches her blanket—their eyes locked together.
How her tenderness to him never ends.
Two days ago acid was thrown on her.
I feel like a corpse, she says through the translator,
but for my child I have to keep on.

Breakup

skating Bryant Park rink with my daughter
after the Newtown murders, December, 2012

Even in Manhattan, skyscrapers
hemming it in, dusk makes a difference
this frozen first week of January.
Look, I urge you, *evening light.*

The utterly clear sky,
still brassed with sun, has ratcheted
one turn toward darkness.
No pink. Something metallic,
the tones of a struck gong.

I'm trying to comfort you
through your breakup: *one door has to close*
before another can open, but it might
not be true, old sayings the finished edges
we design to stop the raveling.

What I know about ice and staying up,
my feet learned years ago on the rough
forest ponds in Montana. The story you remember,
skating miles on Wyoming creeks,
that was my first husband,

chased by the knowledge he was gay.
Didn't he take you with him on the ice?
No. He had to leave me
to make me understand
I couldn't abandon myself.

The frozen wealth of these buildings
shrinks us. Swept around the oval
by the skaters' momentum, I can barely
stay even with you. If you've answered,
I can't hear.

Keeping your child safe.
What are you willing to do for that?
challenge the parents of six-year-old Ben,
mowed down by a crazed man. His killer
once a vulnerable boy himself.

Ben, with his soft cheeks and perfect pitch.
What are you willing to give for your child's
happiness? Holding you these days
after your breakup, like a crackup,
but leaving no visible bruises,
their words make me worry
I've left something undone— it's failure,

and not these reverberations
spreading across the sky, deeper and wider,
filled, yes, with promise—
the one Ben's parents are learning—
brief winter days open, then close.

They switch on the lamp to reveal
his face in the photograph.
He's with them again that moment.

Newtown's parents assume
the work of their grief—
stopping more murders of children.

The day after things ended, you told me,
I dreamed there was water on the ground.
I looked down, and it was the blood
gushing from my heart. Scary,
but for us, still metaphor.

When I catch up, and you're
whimpering: *My heart hurts and hurts,*
I turn to look—as if I could see it, will
its steady beat.

They Start Using Children as Living Shields

the wars: Iraq, Afghanistan, Syria

It could be any sleepover—
staying up way past
their bedtime, playing
hide-and-seek, tickling,
or mid-story, mid-word,
children pause for a minute,
and their eyes, sensing
immobility, close.

Then the parents come
to tuck covers around them.

These children in *Time*,
lie side by side
in their white blanket cocoons,
readied for burial.

If this row of boys and girls
were the only ones taken.

But no, not even one child
to be put in front of a man,
flaunted before a gun,
not one is ok with me.

Shelter

'Do I dare?' and 'Do I dare?'
T. S. Eliot

Reading an article in the Lewiston Tribune, Idaho

The sheriff dares to speak of the young girls, twelve,
who offer themselves—the fatherless girls whose
mothers are husbandless, abandoned,
or abandoning, like houses overrun by flood.

They are looking for a man to love them,
he says. Looking for safekeeping.

From the Internet, he goes on, *from the
magazines, they know how to fashion
themselves to be irresistible,
to offer what will be taken.
At a party,* he is quoted, *these girls go from
man to man, asking to give oral sex.*

And the young men, nineteen, take. The sheriff
dares to feel sorry even for the men: unsure of the law,
unaware what they are taking. *And they
are going to prison for statutory rape,
for indecency with a minor.*

The girls will tell you. No one was forced,
the sheriff dares to say.
All of this was consensual.

The girls think of themselves only as *body*,
as the dark opening of a listing barn,
or as that which is entered because there's room—
since the parents' arms are lost to them,

40

arms which might have closed
around them, absorbed space, as a tree
can hold off rain, taking it
into its branches.

Past twelve, childhood is lost.

I will go to these girls, the newspaper
quotes the sheriff. *I will teach them
to keep their bodies safe,
teach them to teach their parents.*

I believe his kind intent, this sheriff
who may remember his young-man fragility
and no mother to listen.
He's trying to retrieve what he has lost,
what we are all losing.

Here in the newspaper, sheriff, I'm reading
your fervency, letting you wrap it around me,
so it burns away what we already know—
those who have never felt asylum,
can't teach it.

A door opens into a room
bright with firelight and comfortable chairs,
where someone says, *speak to me,
tell me,* and a shoulder friendly
as a harbor's lee, offers what doesn't
have to be returned, closeness
in which the body, imitative,
becomes unassailable,
itself sanctuary.

III

The Extravagance of Our Longing

Salt tears rose from the wells of longing. . . .

—*The Odyssey*
translated by Robert Fitzgerald

Listening to Stone

Cycladic Woman, Athens, 2300 B.C.

The man who carved you vied and gossiped
with his fellow artists, then fell silent,
listening to stone. No language survives you.
Like him, I'm left hearing your shape.

If you'd been made to lie down
with the dead in their graves, arms
crossed under your breasts would make sense,
stilled body drawn into itself.

Upright, you belong to us.
Your belly swells taut. *Hmpf,* says a woman
and comforts her arms on the shelf
her growing baby makes.

Resting them before they're needed,
lifting her child: it's good to keep the self
intact. I lie down and sleep, waking
as inexplicable to myself as you are,

the day calling for shape, for remembrance.
Long eons of our becoming—orangutans
shifting as easily as air moves leaves
in the highest branches—arms want to bridge.

I stand at the glass case and face you,
matching my arms to yours. The bright paint
which gave you eyes has washed away—
how our tears might well up when we meet.

You carry your child's dream
these four millennia, the stone of you
reflecting the shine in pregnant women.
When this child comes,

both of you unprotected,
your arms begin their unfolding,
reaching toward the ground
you must anchor her to.

Patmos

reading The Odyssey *again*

1.

For the first time in our travels,
it's not hard to imagine
Odysseus driven off course.

A north wind churns white water
against beaches and headlands,
scattering the Aegean's surface
in all directions.

2.

One hot day following the next,
we've lazed these island beaches,
slipped into turquoise water
which held us buoyant as the fabled light.

Once the sun dipped into waves,
trees laid down their shadows.
Sand cooled and we left it, slept
in our rented house, remembered

our dreams. Dawn's orange bleached
from the windows before we wound
the narrow maze of cobblestone
between whitewashed walls and found

the baker. His five words of English,
our five of Greek—we carried his rolls
to coffee on the downstairs patio—
heavenly stasis, just our family of three.

3.

Waiting until the moon spilled its gold
into water—as good a reason as any
to sit late and later in our courtyard.
After dinner and wine, to sleep with her
must have seemed Odysseus' only recourse,
beautiful Calypso nothing but kind.

Dawn found her alone. He watched
from his rocky promontory,
cloak wrapped tight, weeping for home.

4.

On our favorite beach, we try to let
another day dissolve without thought,
but wind drives us to the cliff's
small pockets of warmth.

This restless opening and closing
of wings. We get out our maps,
study possible ferry routes, as if, like him,
we need the gods to release us,
Athena, showing him his way.

The Extravagance of Our Longing

The Temple at Bassae to Apollo Epikourios,
containing the first known Corinthian column,
was built by the Parthenon's architect, 5ᵗʰ century B.C.

bassai–bowl between rocky outcrops

To give thanks for a plague's end,
they quarried limestone from nearby hills,
raised their temple where this *bassai* gave way.

All day we've climbed from the sea
on switchbacks carved hillside to creekbed
into untamed Peloponnese. No guard rails.

Our bodies unfold from the car to face
the streaming wind of late afternoon.
September trees flame against the blue.

What confronts us is a huge tent,
sheltering these fragile remains
from frost heaves and acid rain.

We duck under thick guy cables,
step into the dim hush of a space
once Apollo's—built to greet the sun.

Apollo was just with us at Olympia,
his hand draped companionably
on the shoulder of the sculptor who made him.

Here he lost his human form,
abstracted into the first Corinthian column.
Their god escaping them, his carvers

let their marble capital sprout leaves.
Even darkened, even missing the inner
repetition of Ionic,

this massive golden rectangle,
perfectly fluted Doric,
overpowers. No place for us to stay

as the sun slips toward ocean. We linger
outside, in the warmth released
from heaps of sorted stone, then let ourselves

be drawn once more into the windless quiet.
Two millennia have dissolved this belief
and its gods, yet these columns stand.

At the edges of the surrounding sanctuary
built by pilgrims, small depressions,
reservoirs, shelter crocus, spreading

their bright invasion into the sacred.
Like the builders, we want to feel
gods haunt this sunstruck refuge,

but it's the *temple* which holds us,
the extravagance of their longing
unmistakable among its ruins.

Doors

Patmos: Xora (old city)

Unlock the blue door late on a warm night,
step into a courtyard drenched in jasmine
and lemon blossom. Breathe.
These thick, white-washed walls are your refuge.

When you open the door next morning
in the blinding glare of the walled street, *Yasas*—
good fortune on your head—you say

to the few you encounter. Sometimes
they answer, as you turn left, then right, up narrowing
corridors, under arches, through small tunnels.

Punctuated by doors, double doors, enameled blue,
stained and varnished, or doors
which haven't been tended but are locked all the same.

Half a millennium ago, merchants hid their wealth
behind these blank doors.
Pirates swept over the island like tide.

Secret passages still surrender the women's cries
of last resort, as they rushed their children
to the monastery fortress on the hilltop.

Moonlight brushing your balcony with fire
discovered the dead—dashed babies,
clutching mothers, clothes torn from them.

In one merchant's house, now museum, you stumble
through a maze of rooms and courtyards,
arranged to dodge the sun. Rain meant life.

They dug their catch basins into the hills,
lined them with stone, piped the captured water
to each house's buried cistern.
Look down—way down, before your eyes find blue.
These people too lived by chance.

Afternoons, you read and doze in the warm shade
of your veranda. Setting sun means evening's patina.
Let it invite you into the *stoa*,
opening from the dark like a set from *Carmen*.

Your lightest blouse is enough.
You will be served lamb or moussaka,
and your waiter jokes in English.

The tourist boutique across the square,
opened in a corner of one stone building,
is for you. In the shadows village men
laugh at backgammon.

The dim beam of a flashlight guides you
to your door, its knocker a metal hand.
You won't need to take it in your own.
No sound. For a short time,
you still belong here.

Autumn, Second Flowering

at Mycenae and Delphi

i

In a country where stone substitutes
for water, flowers pushed

through September's packed,
sun-scored earth, an unexpected allowance.

I couldn't know the forces which drove them.
I said *beauty,* and stepped into the city.

The great Cyclopean stones,
corbelled to embrace their royal lions,

sheltered crevices flourishing with cyclamen.
I followed the magenta trail.

ii

We climbed Delphi's Sacred Way in early light.
Among the temples and treasuries, ruined places,

under pines, small washes of yellow crocus
magnified the dustless air.

A thousand years people sought this refuge
against the unyielding future.

Pocked remains still manifested that huge will.
These carvers shaped their passion into marble.

Carved to be, the stone, like its subject,
is always becoming, bud opening to bloom

on the strength of fragility and wilt.
It too resists our hunger to possess.

As we passed the theater, light moved
forward, transforming the flowers, the statues,

the columns. We urged each other, *See this. And this.*
Wanting to hold in sight what had already changed.

Grapes

in the pool, Svakia, Crete

1

I tried to be a little fence
around what I could see was coming
when I realized the man
who had stepped into the pool
was German: *this other family
is from Israel.*

He didn't hesitate. He went right to her,
through the water, made the apology
he wanted to make: *my wife and I
were so kindly received in your country.*

And she, *There are some Israelis
who still refuse anything German.*

My own German stumbling: *healing,
that can come with the years.*
But no one in the pool
was even alive during the war.

I wanted to follow
the man from Hamburg
when he got out, explain
what a good thing he'd done.

2

I stayed. We two families,
with our daughters,
swam apart, joined together,
as our languages hummed.

Everyone spoke English.
Hebrew for their family chat.
German mother, Greek father—
children when their parents fled the Nazis.

Countries lost to them,
the Diaspora can only stand
on language's shifting ground.

Once she knew I spoke German,
this mother could say, yes,
her parents *did* escape. *Their* parents,
and uncles and cousins and everyone
died in the camps.

3

And when later she knocks on our door,
holding her plateful of grapes,
it's language she's talking about:
her husband filled with the sounds
of his childhood, offering Greek
to the farmer he's questioning
about which route to take,
until the man, astounded his own tongue
comes from the mouth of a tourist,
says, *take these grapes*
and now we consume them,
sweet as known words.

4

We sit with our new friends over late supper
in the cool of the seaside café.
No language can answer what they tell us
about the Iraq war: their two older sons
already conscripted.

5

North from here, in Xania,
Nazis massed the island Jews for transport.
The sea took them all.
The rest of Crete starved, its produce
shipped north to feed the starving Germans.

A road cuts its cruel swathe through Europe.
We are always on it, sometimes able to speak.

We two mothers didn't have to teach
our daughters German. We chose to—
our love companioning it past degradation,
sounds, luscious to our mouths
as grapes.

Trio Petra: **Three Rocks**

south coast of Crete, Libyan Sea

For an hour or so, an inseparable threesome,
we let the water carry us, almost
to the jutting seastacks, before as one,
we turn and take ourselves back in.

The deception of the deep
turquoise clarity: what do we know
of currents or creatures? Or the rocks,
how some part of them hidden
might blunt or tear us.

We're keeping the unspoken pact
we've made: to take a longer trip,
see more, we sleep in the inexpensive triples,
parents and grown child in one small room.

Nights, with my lamp of insomnia burning,
I pour over *The Odyssey*, determined
to reread the whole book, since the trident god
blows us from port to port
in our own version of hubris.

"Turn off that light," my roommates complain.
"We can't sleep. Bugs are coming in."

When I compare Odysseus' wanderings to ours,
my husband mentions Calypso and Circe.
Even washed up at last, naked and bedraggled,
without a single companion, the wanderer's lucky:

Athena "lent a hand, making him seem
taller, and massive too with crisping hair
in curls like petals of wild hyacinth."
"You see," my husband adds,
"Odysseus had more sex on his trip."

True enough, Telemachus wasn't in the room
as his reunited parents approached the great bed—
though scene after scene,
parents and fledgling, reminds me of us.

As we swam farther on the willing
buoyancy, lifting arms and legs
to keep the water we loved at bay,
our bodies, wanting most of all to touch,
understood we could drag each other to drown
if we got closer.

But we beached on firm sand, cooled, exultant,
the gods playing on our side this time.

Athena slips the wily one in beggar's garb
to Telemachus. When he reveals himself,
"Salt tears rose from the wells of longing in both men
and cries. . . as those of the great taloned hawk."

Homer never lets the required stuff trap him.
He's cheerful about standard phrases
and doesn't shirk at the amount of blood required.
We'd just label this family's troubles *dysfunction,*

but they are the reason Homer writes at all.
Real warmth for him couldn't come from the sea.

Until these three find each other,
fill the wells of longing, he doesn't give in.

with thanks to Robert Fitzgerald

IV

Heartbeat of the Woods

Hunger
When it's your own pain, you notice it.
A bird that sings when you go by.
No road goes far enough—you understand?
And no sound can find the note—
                    —William Stafford, *The Way It Is*

Dieskau

Too late this December morning, wrapped in my robe,
I drove that mile until trees opened to field.
Pink shawled
the horizon, stars faded, along with the comet's leavings,

a ghostly shower after its fiery meeting with the sun.
Now compressed by winter afternoon,
sun angles
around and through fir shadows in ribbons and streamers,

insists against frozen air to turn the car into a momentary
greenhouse, while Dieskau belts out Schubert.
Already brimming
with light, my caravan spills over, his huge middles and lows

building to sudden quiet when he reaches those rarified
high notes, as if he's bumping
against a limit
he refuses, just on the edge of the grieving world,

setting it to spin again. Briefly close, the comet's zooming
into the universe "never to return."
We children of this star
tell our similar stories. I steer toward home,

Dieskau's notes urging me to their journey
as they orbit icy space,
questioning,
then reach back with light's even-handed touch.

Dietrich Fischer-Dieskau began his famous career
singing in an American POW camp after World War II

Exalted

When the hill's light is still brass,
you start out on snowshoes,
lunching at the spot gray jays leave the trees
in wing-flutter and hop to your hand—
scarce graze of their claws—
wild's touch you've waited for.

Heads swiveling side to side, they check
for danger before their polished beaks,
without once invading skin,
dart onto as many raisins as they can carry.
Then the birds whirr away—themselves light.

You trek on, but turn back in time
to reach the hill again by mid-afternoon,
winter sun already dipping
to pour white-gold over the snow—
light completed, fading,
but not yet dusk's steel violet.

In this ripening, shouldering their weighty,
spangled coats, the firs are themselves
revealed, as wings assume air—what spring
will be, sun streaming onto branches,
alchemized green, you—allowed to watch.

Camouflage

Through cedar dusk
above the river flats,
two elk in velvet
stand watch, surrounded,
chest-deep, by sword fern.
My husband
motions quiet.
Then, like bandits
springing an ambush,
the entire herd rises,
thirty cows and calves,
but turning from us,
melts into the ferns
like one creature,
the leathery swords
uncannily moving.
If we try to follow,
we'll get lost,
or mired in the marshes.
Ours, the path cleared,
they to their rhythms
of brown, dun, and green.
How it is when, at a moment
of approach, the hidden
shows itself, then vanishes.
Over the years saying,
Let's go back. That one spot.
As if our glimpse
belonged to geography
or time.

Heartbeat of the Woods

When I say *I love you*, I mean something
different than I did when you first showed me
this ridge, closed as often as we could be
in each other's arms—even apart,
we imagined together.

Now our bodies have to make space
between them for the inevitable wealth
of our conflict and loss.

I've rounded these switches in summer,
tried to embrace how a meadow in full bloom
contains its end.

Spring's a few shooting stars near the creek.
In the grass, if you look, chocolate lilies'
camouflage, yellow-green mottled with deep
brown—secret as the breast of a bird.

Hidden, a grouse matches our hearts' thud
up the pitch of the mountain.

Each day lately, our five-year old worries
a possible new way for us to die.
As we climb, she asks why
she can't see her piano teacher anymore.
How to explain A.L.S.

You turned to me in bed this morning
the way I know you, one minute asleep,
the next folded around me, kissing.
Then our daughter climbed in,

clinging against my back.
"Come over to my house," she begged.

The mother grouse nests on the ground
in a sheltered scrape, raising her chicks alone.
Speckled breast, splotched eggs—
what's vulnerable hidden in plain sight.
She depends on endless shades of ground.

This chocolate lily joins color with grass and sticks,
last year's abandoned leaves.
its six petals nodding earthward.
Inside, on the glowing stamens,
yellow jackets hang.

One switchback after the next takes breath.
Geologically, it's young here.
Who's to say another ice age couldn't
begin anytime? I don't want
to imagine ice closing down slowly
on the houses, smothering this tender Peninsula.

At the top, we three lunch by the clumps
of phlox and windflower, their white
blinding in windy sunshine. We crowd together
for warmth, a solid trio. The view from this spot,
which counts too, holds perfectly clear.

December

Let's get going, haul the tree in.
We're squabbling.
Why should I help you meticulously
brush dead needles from our eight-foot fir,
sprawled in the driveway?
I hate your perfection in small things
while the big ones molder.
A wall against my rain of stones,
you keep stolidly brushing.

From the little bowl of branches
at the top, bulging awkwardly
in an upward spiral, without a word
you hand me a perfect moss nest, animal hair
coiled to cushion eggs—bits of shell,
tiny smears of bird lime left behind
because flight needs no home.

I brush some more, then let you
finish things the way you like.
You hurry. We squeeze the tree
through the front door—
each misstep against walls and
furniture wraps us in fragrance.
Before our lift, I stop us
to settle the nest in place. Both
holding on, we swing the trunk upright.

A Hawk

stooped
like Icarus dropped out of the sky.

Missing small prey on our feeder,
it swept through surrounding salal,
pivoting, first one wing
down, then the other.

Songbirds tumbled from their hiding.
Talons still empty, in thirty seconds
the Cooper's had touched

on the top of the near madrone,
the high point in our far cottonwood,
on into sky.

Behind the kitchen window,
my husband and I called to each other,
See that. Wow. Moves we couldn't fathom.

2
Lately he's made me listen
while he talks of the tides' steady acceleration,
slowing the earth.
It's important, he says, *to keep track.*
Each day's infinitesimally longer.

After so many millennia,
we won't need an extra day
on the leap years.

3

Last month our daughter flew
thousands of miles to us.

Into the void we had learned to fill,
she touched down, scattering order.

Late breakfast, then she climbed
on my lap like a child,
and it was already evening.

Let's drive to the coast, she said.
I need new shoes. Can we eat out?
In their lightness the days expanded—

clear to the ticket counter, through jokes,
checking bags. Until the last good hug.

Behind the security gate she disappeared,
like her waving, into space.

Her dad and I walked
through the empty parking garage
and drove home washed with light,

the cosmos, having emptied it,
bringing the moon full again.

Summer of Flashing Whales

talking to my daughter after a summer of camping,
then seeing King Lear in the round

1. Whale Boat

When the minke surfaces twenty feet
from our boat and its sudden exhaled *huff*
brings us that close,
the sleek silence of its body—like a raven
in flight—vanishes before we can
know to see eye or mouth or fin.

Yet he hath ever but slenderly known himself.
Regan sets the play adrift.
No glimmer of what his daughters need
rises before Lear's blow has glanced
off Cordelia's too-shining face.

2. Elwha River

Sentenced, then father and daughter
find footing on the comfortable love
you and I are often walking.
Trail time, one behind the other,
we're quiet in summer's realized air.

Elusive, what parents owe, how children
might act with grace—

you offer your hand as I once
guided you across the cliffside trail,
teach me to bump over rocks belly flat
when we swim the Elwha's icy rhythm.
None of that pinned down in the three hours
Lear's people stage their heartbreak.

Edgar, the fool, Lear stripped
to underwear, naked madness.
We hide our eyes.

3. Peninsula Beaches
Two grays spouting just beyond
white water at Shi Shi have us sprinting
to keep them in sight. Only that.

The hundred yards of deep which separate us
from them, as necessary
as the fog minkes flash through
while we stare from Kalaloch.

An osprey hovers along Yellow Banks'
crescent, poised to plummet,
then pulls up from the waves into shore spruce—
back and forth, until light ends,

a willing patience Lear learns.
Sing, and tell old tales, and laugh,
taking *upon us the mystery.*
His words.

The wind moans once, rising
into the day's rare sultry heat.
From the west comes gathering cold.

4. South to Oregon
Summer's end, we stroll arm in arm
on Cannon Beach. I was a child here,
my memories too scant to please you.
We marvel the hundreds of seabirds
crowding their nests onto Haystack Rock.
I try to say enough.

How can the mother cormorant
teeter too on the ledge her chicks fill,
their beaks scavenging hers?
She opens the wide cloak of her wings
until the tips touch rock wall:
spread-eagled against basalt, she warms all four.

V

Pearl One

and if I could name this
in a frenzy of understanding
it would be called hunger
that sits in a woman's spaces
        —Lucille Clifton

And yet, I was a living child—
With Food's necessity
Upon me—like a Claw—
        —Emily Dickinson

Pearl One

I languished on the couch, watching Mother
sweep the smooth lines from needle
to needle. *Show me.* Two mismatched sticks
and a dab of leftover yarn. *Knit one row,
then purl it back.* The best part—getting stuck.
Letting the warm air wrap my summer body,
no pressure, while she read the map
of my tangle and unlocked it.

I could use her help tonight, lost
in a pair of Christmas mittens for my daughter.
Even after I knew, I counted purl
as the oyster's rounded layers, *luminosity,*
yet it took me years to understand
that a raised bead signaled a purled stitch.

She purled miles, her even rows
making the knitted outside lie flat and smooth—
a jacket sweater for each of the six men
in our family. I learned enough to make one,
insisting on pure wool I couldn't wear
for the scratch. The sleeves hung inches
too long in errorless procession.

She sat there unmoved, awash
in her yarn and the soft regular tap
of her needles, serenity I envied,
my restless arms and legs growing longer
and longer, stretching out to hug the couch
then crumpled up, nothing about me
compact. She could see the whole.

As I hiked the Soleduck this morning,
our northern sun edged over mountains
to shaft through mist clinging to the big hemlocks.
All afternoon, its wooly globe skimmed
along the rims, never really rising.

In the mix of light and shadow, streams,
their hidden strands purling toward the river,
hugged the lay of the land.
I trusted their arrival.

Big Hole

I will fight no more forever.
                    Chief Joseph

   two brothers and I talk

1.

You're reading Nez Perce history again.

You weren't even born when Mom and Dad
started taking us to the battlefield.
But you push past me to tell a story
when *you* were nine.

The folks began their trek from the Clearwater
to Dillon, *late, disorganized as usual,*
you laugh. They made it over the Bitterroots,
but too tired, no money,
they pulled off at the battlefield—
maybe the only safe place on that wild road—
to sleep in the car until light,

as if they couldn't help imitating
Joseph's Nez Perce fleeing
through those same unforgiving mountains.

You woke to dawn washing over ground
drenched with their families' blood,
women and children dragged from their teepees,
still in sleep, and what?

skulls of infants smashed with gun butts
in front of their mothers—
poor white boys, adrift from the Civil War,

79

taking out on them the rage
Sherman's March to the Sea hadn't assuaged.

In your story, *before breakfast,*
before anything, Dad hauled you
through the exhibits one more time.

2.
I remember the dusks. We are late
once again. No time for dinner, if Dad is to walk
from marker to marker on the disappearing field.
Like you, nine, I elect myself his companion, hoping
he'll notice me. As he stops at each place
a person was killed, he doesn't spare details.

Do you understand? His outrage lights his way.
I am barely visible in the shadows.

3.
We must have gone every year. You're still
talking. *My birthday same day as the battle.*
How green and generous the valley is,
ripe for stealing. All of us kids can see that now.

I don't know if I can face another history
of the Nez Perce War, I say, heartbreak
of a small group of families hunted down by an army,
chased into the snow-bound mountains,
no food, and—our middle brother has waited
for his turn—*making camp only because they thought*
they'd reached Canada. Beaten there.

I've read the book about the survivors,
loaded onto trains south to Oklahoma.
Agents skimmed their government food allotments.

Malnutrition, unheated houses, then TB
finished the killing—a small Auschwitz.

Our words stream against the growing cold tonight,
just like then, but of course we can't know
what they endured, or whether Dad had any idea
why he had to walk the trail each time,
over and over taking those deaths to heart.

We kids had already learned what it meant
to live without protection. We were
tilled ground: another hungry night
on the road. Pressed to the backseat door,
I wept for the mothers and children
Dad had given me.

Along the Columbia River Highway

1

Sunday nights late, reluctant to end a family visit,
highway their metaphor as it carved along the basalt
following the Gorge's own moves,

my parents must have descended
the Rowena Grade, each weekend serpentining
bluff top to river's edge at The Dalles.

They were leaving the lush Willamette
of their childhoods, striking east
into Oregon's bench country,
land barely loosed from volcanic fire.

Moorings no longer mattered
after Kamikaze had torn through Dad's squadron,
and he was alive.
What could they imagine but possibility?

What their many children, what I,
might need, didn't keep them from
spinning their dream clear to Montana
where they set me down
in the brittle wind of the sagebrush plateau.

2

Once, even later than usual,
the state parks full, Dad simply stopped
on the rock-strewn bluff above the river
and pitched our tent in someone's unfenced field.

Mom slept in the car, afraid of rattlers,
but I loved stretching into my bag

after our cramped drive. Star windrows,
then the Army surplus down,
soaked with the day's heat.

Early, before the land owner could find us,
we crawled out of the tent,
scratched through cheat grass to the cliff's edge,
the big solid river below, shouldering through
its landscape of compromise.

3
Grown tall against prairie wind, I escaped
to give my daughter the forgiving northwest coast.
This hot summer night in the choking dust
at Rowena, signs warning of ticks and snakes,
I show her how it was.
Even on unstable ground, longing makes its claim.

Our hotel is waiting; my small family
doesn't have to imagine a place to hold us.
But as we ease down the highway's steep descent,
I'm in the 1950 Chrysler my parents couldn't afford,
lights blazing only a short distance ahead.

Horse Fantasies

for all the horses I didn't get to ride
the years of my girlhood in Montana.
I wasn't Terry Ann, the last child
and only daughter of a rancher
whose spread lay deep
in the sheepland steppe, forty miles
south of our little town.
Terry Ann, whose mother, like all
the ranchers' wives, moved to town
when snow closed the ranch roads,
so her child could go to school.
Alone there, in the cozy house,
lavished what she had on her,
mohair sweater sets and the pleated wool
coordinated skirts I longed for.
Singer in Teen Tones, skier on weekends
she wasn't cheer leading (only in grades
I edged ahead) and summers,
horsewoman with a flair, riding crop,
tooled boots, and barrel racing—
her father, one of the royalty our town
bowed to, tanned, wiry sheepmen,
tainted, yes, of course,
by years of tearing lambs from unwilling
wombs, bossing the dark-skinned men
who sheared. Her father, sorry
for how he'd quarreled with his sons
until they left him,
one to doctoring, the other to drink,
taught her horseflesh, the saddle merely
an extension of four-legged motion.

I spoke the language of those ragged plains
as well as she,
who learned to sweep through them,
wind's love, not its resistance.

Lower Lights

an old hymn:
Let the lower lights be burning
Send a gleam across the way.
Some poor fainting, struggling seaman,
You may rescue, you may save.

As if a universe of black holes weren't out there,
sunset's spread evenly as watercolor, one stripe
of pure mango between ocean and dense fog.

I turn back on this strip of sand, away
from the headwind, to face the faded wool of day's end.
Pt. Wilson Light begins its rhythm, *warning, saving.*

Let the lower lights be burning—Mother's voice
swelled for the chorus as we drove Lake Washington's
shore of dusk-lit houses to pick up Dad from work.

He was her sailor miraculously spared
in the War's cruel shelling. The car's heat hushed
along my five-year-old bare legs, feet shoved into slippers

for the ride. On Whidbey tonight, across the stretch
of inland water, ambulances and squad cars whirl red.
Someone being saved. I seize on the bright panes

of the crossing ferry, even the icy fluorescence
which pours from these park restrooms—
gleams across the way. Gray, the tall windows

of my Kindergarten classroom, the kind eyes,
my teacher questioning why I clung to my chair
and cried. Neither of us could have defined

my yearning to be held. Evenings, Mother and I drove.
She sang her *keeping of the lights along the shore.*
One hand didn't leave the wheel to urge me

from the passenger arm rest toward her. Maybe
she didn't know herself why she couldn't.
After years, I was the one drawing away.

Powwow

talking to my dad

Every Sunday night at story time
you told us kids how your grandfather moved the dresser
by covered wagon from Texas to Oregon—
carried it on peoples' backs when the oxen
couldn't pull the load up a gully.

You didn't explain why that word, *pioneer*,
crossed your lips like a curse
much of your life. While you tried to make up
for what settlers did to the Indians.

You raised us on the powwow circuit,
but when we bedded down in our army surplus tent,
your high, thin voice crooned the old Texas
herding songs—*tumble, tumbleweed.*

All night, willow whistles called,
as the fasting Bannock rose from their pallets
and danced toward the sun pole.
I woke to another day, squatting with you
on the lodge's rush floor, an unwanted white kid.

Sometimes Cowboy Joe, sometimes
Wannabe, you never admitted the person
you were. Taught me the same.

I had to leave that. Leave the horsewoman
I never was, just a visitor
in the Clearwater Valley where you finally
bought your two hundred acres of "ranchland"
across the river from tribal headquarters.

Where are my bags? you worried as your dementia
deepened the schism. *When can I get home?*

I'm asking that question tonight.
My brothers and I crowd into the powwow
long after you're dead. Five hundred *Nimipuu*
jam their ceremony hall, chiefs in full headdress
leading the grand entry. Beside them
in the denim his generation was forced into,
tiny Horace Axtell, ninety, still makes a gesture
toward the steps, his cane helping him.

I read his book: torn from traditional ways,
served up to World War II, alcohol,
then Axtell spent long years in prison.
Once free, he helped rescue
the Nez Perce past, teach self-governance,
ideas I recognized from your years of talking.

As a girl, how carefully I set each footstep
in yours, trying to do things the way
you wanted. You didn't glance back.

That I might have your war inside me
was my job. Explaining to people
who weren't listening that a genocide
had taken place. Explaining to myself
in mind of double loss:
why I was a woman and the wrong race.

A Feast

Dad Visits Me in Port Angeles

> *The rest is silence.*
> > *Hamlet*

This morning he catnapped, waking
to stare hard into the silence. *Betty*, he began.
Where is she? Betty.

He can't remember Mom is dead.
As a girl, I learned that stare didn't reach me,
but turned inward, to the mysterious

disappearance of the Anasazi
or the nature of being. Nothing about
our ontology. He shifts in his chair

and I straighten from weeding strawberries.
He starts over, always a point outside us:
I know these trees.

His true daughter, I test him.
Which ones? That cedar? The madrones?
Sword ferns is all that comes.

I squint into the sun, remembering
how much farther he can see.
A hundred yards away lush clumps hold the bluff.

Betty, will she know where we are?
When I answer, *Most likely,* he drifts on.
You're a good gardener here in the valley.

He means the Willamette of his childhood.
Now I'm asking, *Remember the summer we visited
Grandma, picked strawberries to get gas money home?*

He answers, *I taught you how to garden.*
That was later, in Montana.
He spaded up the prairie as if it were loam—

You take care of the rest.
From dying sods I shook the soil, fruitful
only in symbiosis with its native grass.

When our February sun drops, Dad begins to shiver.
I feel wind across that rattler country,
killing the gardens. We go in.

Betty, where is she? he pleads.
I distract him with apples, naming as I cut—
Burgundy, Winter Golden, King.

Quite a feast, he says. *I ate them
with great deliciousness,*
the way he always wanted to christen an event.

I don't know what we're made into,
he adds, eyes on me.
A good question, I answer.

He Named Your Basket *Harbor Lights*
A Coiled Willow Basket, ca. 1900

at Seattle Art Museum's Indigenous Beauty 2015
Louisa Keyser, Washoe, 1831-1925

Just that I thought your basket represented two words
for safety, but you were reaching into
nothing known, into black water you understood—
weaving "on the northern bank of Tahoe's Truckee
        River outlet."

You crossed the lake each summer to your dealer, you *his*
        discovery.
White women coming to view your baskets
still called you *dirty* in front of you, their way
to appease guilt—settlers stealing land, timber, fish.

Your basket's round shoulders rise from river willow,
its weedy crowding to Western streams.
Onto the ripened surface you've patterned red and black,
red bud and fern root—like him, I could see
miniature shores with flames leaping above them,
water shining them back to us, harbor lights.

Periodic and small, they disclose the walkable land,
telling the night water, as it disappears into shore,
fragrant with deep, of their bright boundary.
People won't stumble and drown.

Next to your basket, the 1907 photo
wraps your tall and bulky body in ill-fitting calico;
only around your waist a beaded belt reminds us,
another custom of clothing still carried beauty.

Louisa Keyser, a "civilized" name for English-speakers.
Datsolalee, your dealer's choice.
From *Sotheby's* to *California Baskets*, each article I read
claims something different: "Your *tribe* gave you Datsolalee,
meaning 'Queen of the Washoe Basket makers.'"
"The name means 'big hips.'"
"The name comes from Dr. S. L. Lee, a white benefactor."

Maybe, as one story claims, *Debuda* was your Washoe name—
"the quiet one," you poised by the water to learn it.

"Fearful to take the journey," you were exhibited
in St. Louis by your dealer. He made your baskets famous.
Harbor Lights, he said.

This photo's caption tells me otherwise:
the ample self of you harbors
two "from your final visionary masterpiece series,"
one indeed *Light Reflected*,
but the other, the one I'm seeing today, you named
Hunting Game of Air in a Proscribed District.

Inside the dress, in other words, mind and heart
brave into nothingness, into the opaque water
of a spirit's drowning, suddenly dropping
beyond your depth—you, instead, afloat, finding, hunting
the game of hunger's satisfaction.

What person daring that place isn't reviled?

Why the basket leaped up at me through the glass case
with its fragment of universe hazarded, claimed.

Closing In

Mom

Sky filled with waving, huge wind in our hemlocks,
then straight-down November rain. The first anniversary
of your death clears to porcelain blue.

Last week I wept, as each of your final days came alive,
the incredible force of you being diminished. Dread
settled on what we couldn't resolve: cherishing each other.

Hoarding this bit of sun, I remember my drives
to visit you through the years—the rush of excitement
each time, that things *could* be different.

Above me, in the mountains, snow falls steadily,
muffling what can be heard. Creatures are deep
in their burrows or have moved to the lowlands.

Even the gray jays rest where lichen grows
in the inner reaches of alpine fir. For me, expectation
begins to unravel. I'm learning that freedom.

Notes to the poems:

This Far Along: This poem is for Lisel.

In Brooklyn: Lines from Walt Whitman are from "Crossing Brooklyn Ferry."

Giving My Daughter *The Scarlet Letter:* The poem is "For a Thirteenth Birthday."

The Extravagance of Our Longing: For more on the Temple, visit http://whc.unesco.org/en/list/392.

Big Hole: When I was small, my family lived in Dillon, Montana; my younger brothers were raised near Lewiston, Idaho, on the Clearwater River. The highway between the two areas approximates the path Joseph and the Nez Perce took as they fled the pursuing U.S. army.

Powwow: The sun dance mentioned took place near Fort Hall, Idaho, among the Shoshone-Bannock Nations in the late 1950's. At this time, fasting was central to the ceremony, but piercing was no longer common practice.

Notes to the poems

About the Author

Hunger is Alice Derry's fifth full collection of poetry.
Her fourth book *Tremolo* appeared from Red Hen in
2012. Tess Gallagher writes of the book: "*Tremolo* is
a tour de force of vibratory power that marks Alice
Derry as having come into her own as one of our very
best poets." *Strangers to Their Courage* (Louisiana
State University Press, 2001), was a finalist for the
2002 Washington Book Award. Li-Young Lee writes
of *Strangers*: "This book . . . asks us to surrender our
simplistic ideas about race and prejudice, memory and
forgetfulness, and begin to uncover a new paradigm for
'human.'" *Stages of Twilight* (Breitenbush, 1986), won
the King County Publication Award, chosen by Raymond
Carver. *Clearwater* appeared from Blue Begonia Press
in 1997. Derry has three chapbooks: *Getting Used
to the Body* (Sagittarius Press, 1989), *Not As You Once
Imagined* (Trask House, 1993), and translations from the
German poet Rainer Rilke (Pleasure Boat Studio, 2002).

Derry's M.F.A. is from Goddard College (now Warren
Wilson). She is Professor *Emerita* at Peninsula College,
Port Angeles, where she directed the Foothills Writers

Series for three decades. In 2013, she helped plan
the 75th Raymond Carver Birthday Celebration and
delivered its keynote address; in 2017, she was Peninsula
College's 17th Writer in Residence. With colleague Kate
Reavey, she has also facilitated writing workshops
for area tribes. She lives and works on Washington's
Olympic Peninsula. Her website is: www.alicederry.com.

9 781936 657292